# THE PINK TIE PRINCIPLE™

The Ultimate Strategy For Smashing
Through Any Business Challenge

By James Ashford

JAMES ASHFORD

3 5 7 9 10 8 6 4 2

First Published 2014
Copyright © James Ashford 2014

James Ashford has asserted his right to be identified as the author of this work in accordance with the Copyright, Designs and Patents Act 1988. The moral right of this author has been asserted.

**All Rights Reserved**

Without limiting the rights under copyright reserved above, no part of this publication may be reproduced, stored in or introduced into a retrieval system, or transmitted in any form or by any means (electronic, mechanical, photocopying, recording or otherwise), without the prior written permission of both the copyright owner and the above publisher of this book

**Acknowledgements**

Every effort has been made to trace copyright holders. The publishers will be glad to rectify in future editions any errors or omissions brought to their attention.

Published by Ashford Enterprises Ltd. Registered in England with Company Registration No: 09174040. Registered Office: 6 The Row, Old Cantley, Doncaster, South Yorkshire, DN3 3QJ, ENGLAND

For more information visit www.PinkTiePrinciple.com

# CONTENTS

| | |
|---|---|
| INTRODUCTION | 5 |
| THE MINDSET | 13 |
| THE PRINCIPLE | 17 |
| STEP 1: PLAN | 21 |
| STEP 2: IDEAS | 37 |
| STEP 3: NEW KNOWLEDGE | 51 |
| STEP 4: TEST | 71 |
| STEP 5: IMPLEMENT | 81 |
| STEP 6: EVOLVE | 95 |
| THE BEGINNING | 107 |
| INSPIRATION | 110 |
| ABOUT THE AUTHOR | 111 |

# INTRODUCTION

If you own or run a business and you're anything like me, you will constantly encounter huge problems. Now you can fluff these up all you like and call them 'challenges' or 'opportunities'. But at the end of the day, these are things that will derail you. These are things you are going to have to smash through and get to the other side of, or you are going to fail.

I don't have enough customers. I have too many customers. I don't have enough money. My cashflow is killing me. My staff are just not on board with where we're going. My customers are a nightmare and sap my energy. I work ridiculous hours. I'm not getting the rewards I deserve for the effort I'm putting in. The list goes on.

Again, if you're anything like me, you've probably been trying to work through these challenges yourself, because you believe they are unique to you and no-one else can solve them. And because you are determined, and persistent, you always find a way… eventually. You always figure a way out, and whether it takes a month or a year, you break through. You don't always know how you get through, but you just do.

But wouldn't it be great if you had a proven strategy that could get you through every challenge you're ever going to face? Wouldn't you feel stronger if you knew that whenever a challenge appeared, no matter how big, how sudden, or what that challenge was, you had a precise method for smashing it out of the way with absolute certainty, in the shortest time and with the least effort?

Whatever your most pressing challenges are, I am going to give you a clear strategy that you'll be able to implement instantly. It will give you the systemized approach you need, to breakthrough to the outcome you most want.

As a business mentor, speaker and trainer, **The Pink Tie Principle**™ is the six-step system that I teach and have repeatedly used to solve any and every challenge, in all sorts of companies. From small, start-up businesses to multi-million pound global organisations, this system solves challenges. It has worked every single time, without fail and I know that if applied correctly, it always will.

## Create Your Success

I have a Masters Degree in Industrial Design. The Pink Tie Principle was born out of the design process and is based on sound creative foundations.

The creative process is designed to solve challenges: whether that's the challenge of designing a new brand for a company, or a new product designed to solve a specific problem. The design process is a robust, proven system, which, if applied with persistence and the belief that it will work, will always lead to the outcome you want

It's a logical process, which looks for answers to the problem. People wrongly think that 'design' and 'creativity' are magical art forms, where a creative genius miraculously produces a wonderful outcome.

I have never thought of design like that. For me, designing and being creative is about working through a logical process to find the answers you're looking for. That's it.

The answer to the problem is always out there, and often staring at you in the face. The art of being creative is knowing where to look for that answer. If you have to 'think' up the solution in your own head, then you're doing something wrong. The answer should always be discovered and can therefore always be justified.

Before I started helping businesses with their overall challenges, I helped them specifically with their branding and marketing challenges.

Let me tell you about a school I worked with. They were working with a branding agency to design their new logo, and despite loads of ideas, they were all wrong. Now this was a big problem because the school had just turned into an academy and was about to open their doors to a new academic year. They needed a brand to go on the children's uniforms, on the signs and on the school bags. They needed a brand to reflect their new aspirations as an academy, but they were a mile away from finding the answer. So, I said to them, right, I will sort this out for you. I will design you a new brand and I will have it finished within 24 hours. They asked me how many designs I would be proposing and I said, "One. The right one."

It wasn't that I was being arrogant; I just knew that the correct solution was out there, and I knew I had the strategy to find it. And in less than 2 hours, I had found their new logo.

The next morning I presented the new brand to the school and they loved it! The brand was a huge success and is now on their signs, letterheads and school uniforms. I'm even more proud to say that my little boy now goes there and wears the uniform and carries the bag, with the logo on it that I designed.

Later on in this book, I will tell you exactly how I arrived at the solution and what the final design looked like, just so you can have a greater understanding of the process I use to solve challenges, fast.

The Pink Tie Principle is the six-step process that I developed to combat the challenge of design problems. Essentially, how do we go from where we are now, to where we need to be? It's a creative process designed to solve any challenge you may face. But you don't need to be 'creative' to use it.

It has been used in many scenarios from "How can we increase our profits by 50% over the next 12 months?" to "How can I get our entire team to be pulling in the same direction, fast, now, today?" From "How can I work less hours and achieve more results?" to "How can I be happier?"

You see, challenges should actually be welcomed because they are the gateways to greater successes. They will never stop coming and nor should you want them to. Because with each challenge you overcome, you become stronger, pull ahead of the pack and take one step closer towards your goals. And these challenges aren't unique to you. Everyone is facing the same challenges. The person or the company that becomes most successful, is the one who solves just one more challenge than everyone else. The one who keeps going.

We all have challenges; we always will. And I promise you that you wouldn't want it any other way. Challenges, problems, whatever you call them, are gifts. And they are there to entice you and lead you forwards and upwards.

So if you're ready to learn the process I use to overcome any challenge; if you want to learn the ready-made strategy that you can use in an instant; and if you're ready to have a system that will prevent you from feeling overwhelmed when challenges arise, then let me introduce you to **The Pink Tie Principle.**

## How This Book Works

Before we start, I just wanted to state that I hate books that are filled with waffley bullshit where you think, 'just get to the point!' You know, those books that could've been written using half the amount of words and still got their message across. The value in a book for me is the ideas it conveys, not the number of pages it's printed on.

I know how busy you are and how little time you have. I therefore promise to get to the point fast and to give you all the information you need in the most concise number of words with none of the waffle.

So if you want a book to fill those lonely winter nights, buy a novel. If you want a straight-talking, practical guide for driving your business forwards at pace and smashing through challenge after challenge, keep reading.

The majority of the examples I will give throughout the book will relate to business, but there will be a few personal ones too to help drive certain points home.

I personally believe that businesses are only extensions of people. I also believe that there are no such things as business problems, only personal problems. So that fact that I use both examples is fine. Let's begin.

"You were born to win, but to be a winner, you must plan to win, prepare to win and expect to win."

Zig Ziglar

## CHAPTER 1
# THE MINDSET

The Pink Tie Principle is broken down into six clear, logical steps, which I'm going to reveal to you now. However, before you take them, it's critical for you to adopt three essential mindsets: BELIEF, PERSISTENCE and PATIENCE.

The strategy I'm going to reveal to you will only work if you approach it with the total belief that it WILL work and with enough persistence and patience to see it through until it does.

The strategy itself can be started in an instant, but the entire process, and therefore results, will not necessarily appear as fast. So when you first implement the strategy, you must begin with total belief that you will arrive at the solution using persistent, pig-headed determination.

This is not a magic wand. It's a strategy. And you must approach it with the unshakable belief that it will work. I already have that belief because I have seen it work time and time again. So borrow mine until you start seeing the results for yourself. Once you start seeing the results, you will own your own belief. Persistence will give you that ownership.

When does a child give up trying to learn how to walk? They don't. When do you tell them to stop trying? You don't. You don't because you have the belief that they will eventually succeed and they have the persistence to do just that.

And when do they start to walk? They walk when they're ready to walk; when the universe conspires to make it so, at precisely the perfect moment. Our only frustration comes from expecting results sooner. You must allow the universe, or whatever you believe in, to act and align itself with your desires. This is where you must have the final mindset; that of patience.

So I will be the parent and extend you my total belief that I know you will soon stop falling and start walking. You just need to have the persistence to get there and the patience until you do.

So if you're ready, let's go.

"A wizard is never late, nor is he early. He arrives precisely when he means to."

JRR Tolkien

CHAPTER 2
# THE PRINCIPLE

**P**lan

**I**deas

**N**ew

**K**nowledge

**T**est

**I**mplement

**E**volve

The Pink Tie Principle consists of six steps:

1. **P**lan
2. **I**deas
3. **N**ew
   **K**nowledge
4. **T**est
5. **I**mplement
6. **E**volve

The remainder of this book will break down each of these strategic steps, into the detail that you, your team and your company need to move forward with certainty.

CHAPTER 3
# STEP 1: PLAN

"Give me six hours to chop down a tree and I will spend the first four sharpening the axe."

Abraham Lincoln

So as soon as you saw the word PLAN, you thought WHAATTTTTT? All that build up and you're telling me to plan. Are you kidding me?

Look, let me introduce you to MY way of planning and exactly what I mean by it. By taking a short amount of time out of the process to PLAN, you will end up saving massive amounts of time, heartache and money in the future.

When I think of planning, I always think of planning a journey. Instead of the word PLAN, I should have actually written the words PLAN THE JOURNEY, but that would have messed up my PINK TIE acronym.

This journey planning stage is broken down into four critical parts and you cannot miss out a single one. They are:

**A.** Where are you now?
**B.** Where do you want to be?
**C.** Why are you going there?
**D.** Is that where you really need to go?

## A. Where are you now?

It seems like such an obvious and trite question. Where are you now? But this question is absolutely critical if you stand any chance of reaching your destination. Where are you now? Where EXACTLY are you now?

Let's assume you're going to visit a friend. So you know where you're going and you've been given the exact route to get there. Brilliant.

So the directions are for you to pull out of your driveway, turn left and drive for two miles. Then turn right and continue down that road for another ten miles, then turn left again. Perfect. However, this only works if you know EXACTLY where you are now. Not an approximation. Not where you were last year. Not where you'd like to be. Where you are now.

You have absolutely zero chance of getting to where you want to go, unless you know where you are now. And this is exactly the same when it comes to solving challenges in your business and your life.

Unless you can be totally honest with yourself and those around you about the true nature of the challenge you're facing, you will never be able to solve it.

Maybe you don't know the full extent of the problem. Maybe that's the problem. Maybe you will have to gather some more information to understand it clearer. Whatever you need to do, get the FACTS.

Tony Robbins explained this to me very clearly when he said:

"See things AS they are. Not WORSE than they are. Not BETTER than they are. Just AS they are."

This is the first and most critical step of our journey to solving the challenge we're facing. Let me explain this with a few examples.

**I Don't Have Enough Time**

Nearly every client I work with tells me that they don't have enough time. Who does? So the first step to solving this problem is to understand where your time is going. You might think that you're spending all of your time doing one thing, when actually it's spent doing another.

Incidentally, most people's time is wasted through interruptions: interruptions of emails, phone calls, and people asking irrelevant questions. There's a great book called Rework by Jason Fried, where he explains that working is like sleeping. It's only when you're in deep sleep (REM) that the good stuff happens. When you're woken up, even if only for a second, it can take you 15 minutes or more to get back into deep, meaningful sleep. It's the same with work. Those 1 minute interruptions will actually snap you out of your flow for 15 minutes or more. You only need 4, 1-minute interruptions in an hour, and you will have got nothing of any importance done.

So if you needed more time, one of the first things I would do, would be get you to carry out a time log for a week, so I could first assess where your time was going. (You can download a free

Time Log from my website if you want one – www.JamesAshford.com/free).

Another thing I might do, would be to observe you in action to understand where your time is being lost. I have no chance of improving your situation unless I first understand it. And neither do you.

**I'm Too Fat**

Now I know this isn't business related, but it perfectly illustrates this point. A friend of mine is clinically obese. He came to me, to see if I could help him lose weight. When I questioned him, it was a miracle he was overweight at all, because he played football twice a week, and according to him, he hardly ate a thing. I explained that you don't get to 22 stone by not eating anything.

So the first thing I asked him to do for one week was to use his phone to photograph everything he put into his mouth. Any food, snack or drink. Then after the week, we would know what the actual problem was and could start to work out a plan to solve it.

He never took one photo. His unwillingness to figure out where he was, meant there was nothing we could do to improve his situation.

Instead he bought a gym membership, which was great, and certainly a potential route to a better body. But his unknowing of where he was to start with, rendered this membership useless.

**We Need More Money**

This is another common challenge a lot of businesses face. But before I can begin to solve this challenge, I need to understand EXACTLY where they are now. What do your finances look like? What are the exact figures? (They don't lie). Where is the money being spent, lost or wasted? Why isn't there enough coming in? Let me see the numbers and we'll be able to work out the best route to resolving the problem.

There is no point in bringing more money in whilst there are holes in the boat. It will only serve to sink the boat when you're further out to sea. Block up the holes first. Make the boat float before launching it with more money. Does that make sense?

A good friend of mine is an Insolvency Practitioner and closes down many failing companies. He explained to me that one of the biggest reasons for failure is because of business owners failing to face the facts. They imagine things are better than they are, and only when it's too late are they forced to face the cold hard truth.

The number one reason for businesses failing is because they don't know where they are. Isn't it amazing that just knowing where you are now is the first step towards solving all your problems?

**Action Point**

Whatever the challenge is you're trying to solve, know where you are now. 'See things AS they are. Not WORSE than they are. Not BETTER than they are. Just AS they are.'

If you can't do this objectively because you're too close to the problem, you may need to bring someone in to help you to see things more clearly. Whatever you need to do, answer this question before you move on, otherwise NOTHING else will work.

Ask your staff. Ask your customers. Ask your accountant. Get an independent audit. Discover the truth. Having a gym membership whilst your still stuffing your face with the wrong food just can't work.

## B. Where do you want to be?

This question is simpler. Where do you want to be? What do you want the outcome to be? What is the result you want?

The challenge that most people have is that they focus on what they DON'T want, and spend no time defining what they DO want. So my client's might say "I want my staff to stop being so lazy." This isn't actually what they want. This isn't an outcome. It is not a destination. Going back to the journey analogy again, it's like somebody asking you where you want to go to, and you answer by saying where you DON'T want to go.

In the same context, the better answer to this question would be, "I want my staff to work to their maximum efficiency whilst enjoying the process." This is far clearer in terms of where you want to be.

The other mistake that people make in answering this question is being too vague. Again, going back to the journey analogy, it's like somebody asking you where you want to get to and you respond with "the North." Whilst true, it's not accurate. If you were going on a journey, you would know the exact coordinates and not only that, you would know when you want to arrive.

If you say to me that you need more money, I could say here's a pound, problem solved. Likewise, if you said I need £10,000 but didn't attach a date to it, we could put a 50 year plan in place to achieve it, but that would be no good either.

A more accurate response to the question would be, "We need £10,000 by the end of the month."

**Action Points**

So to recap. Where do you want to be? Not where you DON'T want to get to, but where you DO? And by when? For example:
- I want £10,000 additional income within 30 days
- I want my staff to work 100% more efficiently as a team, and enjoy the process
- I want to have a positive cash flow within 3 months
- I want 10 new VIP clients over the next 12 months

Whatever you want, be clear, be positive and know WHEN you want it.

## C. Why are you going there?

Can you remember what I told you about persistence? The type of persistence that would allow you to walk over hot coals and run through walls for what you want? Well if you want to have enough persistence to see you through to a successful outcome, then you need to know WHY you're doing it. So why do you want to get there?

Knowing why gives you your motive, and once you have your motive, you have your motivation. And your motivation is the fuel for the journey.

If your 'why' is because your accountant told you that you needed to make more money, then it probably won't provide you the persistence you need to see this journey through to the end. If your 'why' is because it will make everything you've ever dreamed and desired come true, then you're more likely to smash through this challenge and get over the line.

You've got to find YOUR 'why'. Why are YOU doing this? It's no good if it's somebody else's reason why. It has to be YOURS. You have to know it deep down because there will be moments on this journey where it gets tough. You will hit traffic. You will get a flat tyre. You will have to walk the rest of the journey in bare feet. The point is, your reason 'why' has to be strong and it has to be yours. Because it's during the tough moments when you're going to have to dig deep and find that next level of persistence to see you through to the end.

You can get through this challenge. You WILL get through this challenge. But you've got to know YOUR reason why.

## D. Is that where you really need to go?

This is probably the toughest question to answer on your own. It's the one that requires the most probing and testing.

The reason why it's the toughest question to answer on your own is because you may believe with your entire being that it definitely is the destination you need to get to. You KNOW your challenge. You KNOW where you want to go. You KNOW your reason why. But before we set off, we must ask this question. Let me tell you why.

If Henry Ford were to have taken people through this process, it would have gone something like this:

**Henry:** What's the problem?
**Customer:** Our horses are too slow.
**Henry:** So what's the outcome you want?
**Customer:** Faster horses.
**Henry:** Why?
**Customer:** So we can get to places quicker.

But Henry didn't aim for that destination. He stopped and asked this question: Is that where I really need to go? Do you really need faster horses? And because he asked this question, he came up with a better answer.

Admittedly, this is tricky. But the clue comes from the previous question: Why?

If you can really understand somebody's 'why', you can use that answer to interrogate the destination. Let me give you a few examples of the destination that people 'think' they want to get to.

**We Need More Money**

Whenever a business owner says they need more money, I always ask "Really?" And it's amazing how often they don't. Sometimes a business owner can think that they need more money, but what they actually need is to stop hemorrhaging it at the rate they are doing. Whilst an injection of cash may appear to solve the problem, I would be asking how they got there in the first place.

It might be that they need to renegotiate payment terms with their suppliers or customers. It may be that they need to charge more.

A better destination for you instead of 'needing more money' would be: we want to be financially sound and highly profitable. That's what you really want. And having THAT as a destination will solve all of your problems, not just your short term ones.

**We Need More Customers**

This is another classic destination that people want to get to because they believe it will make them more money. And while of course you need more customers (everybody does), it may not be the immediate destination you need to get to.

Getting new customers is expensive because you've got to invest money and time in finding them. You then spend even more money and time developing the relationship with them, to get them to the point where they want to buy from you. I would be asking:

- Do all of your existing customers know everything you do?

- Are all of your existing customers spending as much with you as they could?
- Could your existing customers spend more often with you?

So rather than state that you want more customers, a better destination might be: we want to maximize our profits from our existing customers and THEN seek to bring more customers in.

It's far easier to sell to existing customers than it is new ones. And if you are only making 50% of what you could be from your existing ones, wouldn't it make more sense to sell to them first, and THEN to bring in new ones?

Optimise THEN maximize.

**We Need To Get Rid of That Member of Staff**

Everyone has staff problems. Always have, and always will. You may have a member of staff who's a massive pain in the arse and who you would like gone. And they may well be a massive pain in the arse, and it may well be better that they go. But are they the real problem? Is that the best solution?

Again, I would be questioning you and ask:

- Have you defined your core values and culture?
- Do you employ and fire people around those values?
- Have you procedurised all of their key tasks?
- Do you provide regular training to staff?

- Do you carry out regular performance reviews and allow them to review you?
- Have you asked your staff what their problems are?

It is so easy to blame a member of staff, but I would want to know how they became a problem. Did you employ the wrong person? Does your recruitment process need looking at? I don't know. But my point is that you may have a system that produces bad staff; that turns diamonds into coal, rather than the other way round.

So the destination you're looking for in this instance is: we want to build a positive team with a family spirit. And actually, if you were to reassert this as your true destination, and they ARE the wrong person for your team, the chances are they'd jump ship before you arrived anyway

Can you see the importance of interrogating the destination? Is that REALLY where you want to go? My advice would be to look at the bigger picture; the longer term goals.

My daughter is only 3 and suffers with eczema. The doctor prescribed creams and lotions and potions to cure it, and whilst it would clear up for a while, it would just reappear somewhere else. You see, we were trying to solve short term problems and not thinking about the real destination. What we really wanted was for our little girl to have healthy, pain free skin forever more, with little or no effort. As soon as I chose that as the goal, I looked into it more deeply and discovered that she was intolerant to milk. I switched her over to Soya milk and her eczema disappeared.

Question YOUR destination. Think big. Think long term. Think of the best outcome imaginable. That's where you want to be heading.

## A recap on Step 1: Plan

- Take time to plan. It may save you a lot of time, money and heartache in the future.
- Discover EXACTLY where are you now. Or another way to put this is, what is the actual problem? Don't see it worse or better than it is, but actually as it is.
- Find out where you want to get to. Be precise. Find the outcome that you DO want, not that you DON'T want.
- Know why you are going there. You've got to know your reason why, otherwise you'll run out of gas en route.
- Question the destination. Is that where you really want to go? Think long term. Think big. Think best.

Now we know where we are, where we're going and why we're going there, it's time to start making progress. We need to start building momentum straight away and take immediate steps towards our goal.

CHAPTER 4
# STEP 2: IDEAS

"What simple action could you take today to produce a new momentum toward success in your life?"

Tony Robbins

You have the plan in place. You know where you are and where you want to get to. You know why you need to go on this journey and you're happy that it's worth your effort and the correct destination. The trick now is to start walking.

Before you do anything else - before you start 'researching' or talking to people - just start walking.

How can you take at least one step closer toward your destination? There's a great saying from Theodore Roosevelt, which is 'do what you can, with what you have, where you are.' What knowledge do you have already to take just one step closer to where you need to be?

For me, this is a very empowering part of the process because it says ok, I may not have all the answers, but I have some. I can't make it all the way on my own, but I can make a start. And this is an important step because the universe sees that you're playing your part and it will be prepared to meet you half way.

"You don't have to be great to start, but you have to start to be great."

Zig Ziglar

Now I know what you must be thinking – 'If I had the ideas, why the hell would I need this book?' But let me assure you, you have more ideas than you think. So let me help you to get some of those ideas out of your head so you can make a start on that journey.

The first thing is to remove yourself from where you are now. So wherever the problem is, for example your office, get out of there. Change the scenery. If there are negative people around you, move away from them. Get up. Get moving.

## Brainshaking

Right, now it's time to do our first brainshake. A brainshake is like a brainstorm, but not quite as violent. Also, I want to take you away from the negative association of brainstorming sessions, where we all sit round a table and essentially tell everyone how crap their ideas are.

Brainshaking is a phrase I came up with to describe brainstorming without the judgment. It's about emptying our heads onto paper and letting the ideas land where they may. There is no judgment; no good or bad labels being applied. We are only interested in ideas.

The reason we need to remove judgment is because idea 1 might be crap. But it might lead onto ideas 2, 3 and 4. Now 2 and 3 may also be quite bad but you know what, 4 has legs. And when 4 turns into 5 and then 6?!? Now we're talking! But 6 would never have happened if you had said No. 1 was crap. So don't judge.

But worse than this, when you start judging ideas as they hit the paper, you're actually judging the contributor's ability to come up with ideas. And with each judgment, you actually kick them deeper into their cave, where they'll eventually sit, in silence. This is because they stop thinking that it's their ideas that are bad, and wrongly assume that it's their ability to come up with ideas, which is bad. So they just stop. You end up killing the golden goose just because they laid a couple of duff eggs. Forget about the eggs at this stage and nurture the goose.

So can you see how the judgment of the ideas is what kills the creative process. So stop it. There's plenty of time for judgment later, although it won't be done by you.

So sit on your own, or surround yourself with your closest allies. Get a BIG sheet of paper (now is not the time to restrict your thinking) and a big felt tip pen (now is not the time for detail) and start brainshaking. Just empty your heads out onto the paper. Start with the belief that you HAVE the answer. Somewhere in there lies the £million answer, just shake that baby out!

## Stuck for Ideas?

It's likely that you will get stuck for ideas. This is probably one of the reasons you are where you are in the first place, right? So let me help you to get those creative juices flowing so we can unleash the answer. Now don't forget, we don't need to uncover the entire route towards the outcome, we're just looking to move away from where we are and to move closer to where we want to be.

The trick here is to start focusing on different things. And we change what we focus on in an instant with the questions we ask.

So it stands to reason that if we can ask ourselves better questions, we'll have a better focus and should therefore arrive at better answers (I must thank my mentor, Tony Robbins, for teaching me this, who is incredible. Read all of his books, buys his audios, watch his videos and if you ever get the chance, go and see him. He is a brilliant man and has inspired me so much. I can actually say with great certainty that he has changed my life!)

So here goes. Ask the questions with certainty that you'll find the answer and exhaust each one before you move onto the next.

- If we absolutely had to solve this problem within the next 24 hours, what would we do?
- If we absolutely had to solve the problem *completely* within 10 minutes, what would we do?
- If we only had £10 to solve this problem, what would we do?
- If money weren't a problem, what would we do?
- If I were Sir Richard Branson, what would I do?
- How would a classroom of primary school children solve this problem?
- How would Superman solve this problem?
- If we were our largest competitor, what would we do?
- If I just bought the company today, what would I do?
- If we knew we couldn't fail, what would we do?
- What is in fact wonderful about this problem?
- What could we learn from this problem?
- Why is this problem our greatest gift?

Another way to interrogate your problem is to turn the problem itself into a positive question.

So if your problem was: 'my staff are lazy'. You would turn that problem into a positive question and ask: "How can I motivate my staff instantly and forevermore?"

If your problem was: 'we need more money', your new question would be: "How can we create a constant flow of cash into our business with little effort, starting now?"

Can you see that just by focusing on a question rather than the problem, gives us a much greater chance of getting to the outcome we desire?

These are some positive questions you could ask yourself to switch your focus. But it can also be helpful to ask negative questions as well at this stage. Not that we want to think negatively or want negative outcomes. But by adopting opposite mindsets, it can force our brains to dislodge the answers we're looking for. This forces you down different routes that you never thought of. And it's not that those routes are places where you want to go, but what if they were shortcuts to your ultimate destination? So try these questions too:

- If we wanted the problem to get worse, what would we do?
- If we wanted our business to completely fail within a week, what would we do?
- If we were being greedy, what would we do?

- If we were being super cautious, what would we do?

This idea of adopting different mindsets to overcome problems was introduced to me by Edward de Bono in his amazing book `Six Thinking Hats`. De Bono is the father of lateral thinking, and I'll explain exactly what that is and how you can use it in the next chapter.

## Conduct a fake interview

I had originally left this section out of the book for fear of wanting to sound loopy, but here goes.

When I'm driving in my car, alone, and I have a problem, which I'm trying to solve, I have been known to turn the radio off and conduct a fake interview with myself.

So I pretend I'm being interviewed on TV by a famous business journalist or chat show host. They're carrying out an interview about my incredible rise to outrageous levels of success. They then ask me about the current problem I'm trying to overcome. So I just sit and fantasize about ways I overcame the problem and how amazing it was when I broke through this challenge. I also explain how my success was accelerated on the other side of the problem.

Now this may seem crazy, but it helps you to see yourself on the other side of the problem. It tells your mind that you DO get through the problem, and therefore forces the mind to start filling in the gaps between where you are now and where you will end up. It forces it to start finding a solution.

Try it before you go to bed and let your sub-conscious, sleeping mind go in search of the missing blanks. You may be amazed at what it discovers.

## Where do I go now?

Now this idea process might have been so successful that it has taken you all the way to the outcome you wanted. In which case, you can skip the next chapter – New Knowledge – and go straight into Testing.

But let's assume that the ideas process has simply taken you forward, but not all the way. It's time to acquire New Knowledge. You see, you already had a few stepping stones locked away in your mind, which have enabled immediate progression. Now that you have exhausted that knowledge, the trick is to get New Knowledge to generate more stepping-stones that will take you even further forward.

"Do what you can, with what you have, where you are."

Theodore Roosevelt

## A recap on Step 2: Ideas

- Brainshake and don't judge what comes out
- Ask yourself better questions to prompt better answers
- Ask opposite and illogical questions to provoke ideas
- Assume you're on the other side of the problem already

CHAPTER 5
# STEP 3: NEW KNOWLEDGE

"Help only comes to those who ask for it."

Albus Dumbledore

So you've gone as far as you can towards solving your challenge and reaching your goal, and now you've stopped. You've stopped because either you can't seem to access the answer within, or you're without it. So if it's not within, we need to go out, and find that answer from somewhere else.

Now this step seems so logical to me, but it's amazing how many people either don't ask for help or don't know how to ask for help. Maybe it's because they don't want to come across as weak. Look, I was one of the brightest kids in school, but I was only bright because I kept asking questions. I wanted to know the answers and I didn't care how stupid my question was. As a wise man once said, there's no such thing as a stupid question, only a stupid answer.

Answers are all around you. New knowledge is all around you, and I see this knowledge as stepping-stones that will get you closer to your goals. Some people call this stage 'research', but that seems academic to me. I want the knowledge that's going to take me to my outcome as fast as possible.

The other incredible part of this process is that when I arrive, I will own this knowledge. I will have grown. I will be better.

Reaching the goal itself is not what's important here. The MOST important thing in this whole process, is who you become as a result of achieving your goal. So let me tell you where I go to acquire my new knowledge, so you can go and find your own.

## Start At The Heart

The strategy we're going to take, is to move out from the centre. We are going to start at the heart of the problem, with the people we assume would have the most knowledge. Once we've exhausted that, we are going to go further and further until we get what we need.

Now can you remember when you started this book, I asked you to have belief? This is one of those times when I need you to believe. The answers ARE out there; we just need to find them.

This is the very essence of the creative process for me. It's not about conjuring up the answer; it's about finding it.

## Ask Your Executive Team

Step one is to get your Executive Team involved in the process. What do they know? How can they help you? Now you might call these your Director Team, or your Leadership Team, or your Management Team. The point is that this relates to the highest level of individuals you already have in your organisation. Start at the top and get them to contribute together. Take them back to the brainshaking stage and remember not to judge their ideas. These guys might have the answers you need. Listen to them and get them shaking their brains.

## Ask Your Staff

You now need to engage your staff, starting at the top and working all the way down. You might be struggling with an issue, and the cleaner of your building has the answer. You will never know unless you have a strategy in place for getting their feedback. You may be amazed at what they feed back to you.

Very often, business owners and leaders think their staff don't really care or want to contribute to driving the business forward. Many business owners and leaders are very often surprised at what they hear.

There was a TV program a few years ago in England called "Can Gerry Robinson Fix the NHS?" Sir Gerry Robinson went into a failing hospital to try and reduce their waiting list. One of their problems was their struggle to process the number of operations they needed to perform. This led to increasing waiting lists and pissed-off patients. The management teams didn't know what to do, and so Sir Gerry went and asked the nurses who were working on the front line. Their suggestions were fantastic. They knew of unused rooms that could be easily converted into operating theatres and other amazing ideas for solving the problem. The really amazing thing was that management had never even asked them. In fact, the high-level management team had never even met or spoke to some of the nurses.

Isn't it amazing that such a wealth of knowledge could exist within reaching distance and it was never unlocked?

I've got a friend who runs a building company. He was struggling with some major challenges in his business. So I asked him to talk to his laborers, to find out what answers they had. He initially refused because he didn't think that they cared, and even if they did, what would they know anyway? He was wrong. So now, on the last Friday of each month, they have what he calls Tool-Box-Talks, and the ideas he continues to get, massively move his business forward.

## Ask Your Customers

Once you've run out of your own people, we need to get new answers from people further afield. So start with your top customers. These are people who trust and like you and both enjoy and benefit from the service you provide to them. They want you to succeed. They need you to.

So if you were having cash flow problems, do you think it would be reasonable to go and ask your customers for ideas on how you could solve the challenge? And if not why not?

Now you have to pick the right customers; the ones you have a close relationship with. You might be surprised at how they can help you to think of new solutions.

I was working with a client who had the challenge of getting more business in through the door. He had tried traditional marketing and it had cost him a lot of money, a lot of time and he'd got little results from it. I asked him to go to his top 10 clients and ask these two, direct questions:

- Are we getting all of your business?

- What could we do to get you to spend more money with us?

Now these are very direct questions and not suitable to ask every client, but do you know what happened? Within a month, they had picked up over £100,000 of business, without spending a penny on marketing.

Why start trying to attract money from new customers who don't yet know you and don't yet care about you. If you want more money, go and ask your existing clients how you can get more of theirs. It seems so simple doesn't it? But the answers are there, just go and ask.

## Ask Your Suppliers

Suppliers can be an incredible wealth of knowledge for these important reasons:

- They know the industry
- They will be dealing with other companies like yours
- They have an obligation to give you their time

A few years ago, a guy who is now my business partner, had a great idea. He was a plasterer and wanted to get more business. As a plasterer he had to buy insulation. So he went to his supplier and asked this genius question: "Who buys most insulation from you?" And the supplier told him.

He then asked, "What do they do?" The supplier told him that this company insulate and plaster the inside of conservatory roofs to turn them into proper rooms. He never even knew that this industry existed. So he carried out further research (acquired more new knowledge) and found that it was a very profitable, emerging market.

He approached me, we set up a business insulating conservatory roofs and created a very profitable and successful company off the back of it.

This all started because he had the challenge of needing more work and didn't want to be working as hard as he was (he had 4 children under 5 years old at the time. WOW!)

He now works one day a week, *on* the business and not *in* it, makes more money than ever before and has tea with his family every night. All this happened because he asked his supplier that question.

What questions could you ask your suppliers? What are you waiting for?

## Ask Your Competition

Now you might be thinking WHAT???? Ask my competition? Really? Have you lost your frickin mind?

Yes, ask your competition. Now there are a few ways you can do this, depending on who your competition is.

One way might be to do it undercover. Find out who the most successful competitor is that you have and get the new knowledge you need from them. You might have to get them out to give you a quote. You might find out who their customers are and go and ask them your questions. Keep it legit of course, but go and get the info you need to help you.

You may also have some super large competitors who might be willing to give you the information you need, because they don't see you as a threat.

If you were a local restaurant and you went to speak to the franchisee of your local McDonalds, he's not going to see you as a threat. He may be more than happy to sit down with you and give you some pointers.

You might be surprised that very large business owners are actually very happy to mentor and help smaller ones. You've just got to be ballsy enough to knock on their door in the first place and ask for help. Now this idea might require the greatest levels of persistence, but if you decide that you're going to speak with somebody, then go and speak with them. I don't care who it is. If it's Bill Gates, then do what you need to do to get a coffee with him. I'm serious! What have you got to lose? He drinks coffee with someone, somewhere. Why not drink coffee with you for ten minutes? At least get him on the phone.

I'm really serious about this. This kind of action is possible, if you want to make it happen. Look, humans have invented flight; they've invented the light bulb; and they've invented space travel. Humans are capable of incredible things. I'm just asking you to talk to a big hitter. I bet if you're life depended on it you could. Just try it as a game; as a laugh. What have you got to lose? Just decide who you want to speak to, get the phone number of their office, call up and ask to speak to them. Ask for them by first name, use a deep, serious voice and have a tone that might suggest you have some important news for them.

"Hello, can I speak with Bill please? Just tell him it's James Ashford."

"Certainly, I'll connect you with Mr. Gates now."

Call with the certainty that you'll speak with them, I dare you. The only thing stopping you is your limiting belief that wonders why anyone in their position would give you their time. See them as your equal. See them as a partner in your fight to succeed. They were in your position once and they will really admire you for asking for help. My question to you is: which person could you call right now, who could change everything for you? In fact, that is a great question to ask every single day. Who could I call today who could change everything for me? Get into the habit of just picking up the phone and making the call. You can either do this on your own or with help from those who know better than you. I know which option I'd prefer.

The next level of competition is that in a different country. I have a client who is running a successful soccer academy in the UK and growing it nicely. He is looking to franchise out his business and needs new knowledge. There is a much larger business in the USA, doing something similar and already franchising. Through social media he has acquired the owner's name and his speaking with him about the best way to do it.

They're not a threat to each other. Why wouldn't you ask for their help? Again, what have you got to lose?

Now this approach requires persistence and I know what you're thinking – "I can't get him to talk to me." Or "I've tried emailing her already, and she never got back to me?" Look, if you want to get somebody to speak to you, get them to speak to you:

- Connect with them on social media.
- Call them, every week. Every day if need be.
- Keep a positive attitude at all times.
- Send them gifts.
- Sponsor them.
- Send donuts.....every week....for a year!
- Commission a song to them.
- Send a dance troupe to perform in their car park.
- Shoot a video on your phone and post it to them.
- Hand write them a letter.

Do that. THEN come back to me and say you can't get hold of them. But not after one email. Be passionate, be positive and be persistent.

## Ask Another Industry

You may be operating over here in one industry, but there may be an industry over there, with some parallels. Maybe you have a challenge with getting your clients to commit to 12 month contracts. Which other industries use 12 month contracts? What could you learn from them? Who could you go and speak to?

I have a client who turns over many millions and has a large sales team on the phones, who receive a monthly bonus. They're having problems with the way the bonus is structured as it doesn't quite align with the goals of the company. So we looked at the largest companies on the planet who have sales teams on the phone. These companies are turning over £billions. Do you not think that they might have the answer?

McDonalds have a huge challenge of knowing what they can charge for their products in any given country. They spend a fortune on understanding exactly what they can charge, in order to maximize their profits. They have to investigate what the country earns as a whole, what individuals earn, what they spend on other products and what's important to them. This is the only way they can figure out the exact price they can charge for a Big Mac.

Fairy washing up liquid have the same challenge in that they need to know what they can charge for a bottle of Fairy in any given country. But do you know how THEY do it? They take the price of a Big Mac, stick it into a formula and it gives them their answer. Simple.

If you have a challenge that is already being solved in another industry, why reinvent the wheel in yours?

## Consult Books, Audio & Video

Books are an incredible way to gather new knowledge. The average person reads just one book a year, if that. Leading business owners read a book a week, or more.

I personally prefer audiobooks and videos because I can get through a lot while I'm driving or working out. At the time of writing this I'm 35 and reading a book (or equivalent) a week. So by the time I'm 55, I will have read 1000 books. Now I must be more valuable, and capable of solving more challenges in the world after that lot.

Books, videos and audios are created by people who've already been there before. Get their knowledge and save the pain and years of heartache and struggle.

At the back of this book is a list of resources that have inspired me, from books to individuals. Check them out and you will have a constant source of new knowledge in your life, which will keep driving you forwards.

When I discovered this, the results and enjoyment I started getting out of life increased exponentially.

## Get a Coach

A business coach or mentor can be fantastic source of new knowledge. If you choose the right one, they will be able to guide you through the challenges you're facing and towards successful outcomes.

When I work with a new client who's never had a coach before, they will often take some convincing initially because they think :

- We can't afford it
- What can you tell me that I don't already know
- I don't have time for a coach
- We'll just muddle through this challenge ourselves.... again.

All of these answers make no sense, and once I start coaching my clients, their only regret is that they didn't start sooner. They end up making more money, get more time back and have someone in their corner, fighting their challenges with them.

A great coach is a valuable person to have on your team, whether you work with them every week or every quarter. Find someone who you can get on your side to guide you through the challenges you're facing and to hold you accountable for doing what you said you'd do.

## Use Lateral Thinking

All of the other approaches require deep thinking. You are going deeper and deeper into one channel of knowledge. Moving over to another industry is your first lateral step, but it's only a small one because it's still within the sphere of business.

The phrase 'lateral thinking' was first used by Edward de Bono and means that rather mine for new knowledge within the hole you're already in, you're going to find a new hole somewhere else and then connect the two together.

So for example, I'm a second Dan Black Belt in Goshinkwai, which is a kick-ass martial art. There is new knowledge I've acquired there, which I apply in my businesses and with my clients. That's lateral thinking because I've taken two completely different sets of knowledge and connected them together. Let me give you an example.

When you're throwing somebody, you must maintain good balance throughout the throw and cannot lean on or rely on your opponent for support. The test for this is that at any point throughout a throw, if you were to press the pause button and your opponent were to disappear, you must remain standing solidly. You need to have a strong base at all times and a robust stance. Opponents can fall, slip out of your hands or anything, but that shouldn't put your position at risk.

So I apply this philosophy to business. I have the mindset that at any point, a member of staff, supplier or customer could just disappear and you must remain standing.

If a customer disappeared, you must ensure you have sufficient monies from them at that point, so as not to be out of pocket and therefore exposed.

If a member of staff were to disappear at any point, you must be able to replace them with little disruption. So you need a great recruitment process, training system and solid procedures to guide the new recruit in their new role.

So can you see how just that one martial art's philosophy can be used to solve business challenges? The answers are all around you, but only if you're looking and willing to connect them with the problem you're facing right now.

Where can YOU go for lateral thinking? Anywhere. You can look for new knowledge absolutely anywhere.

Let's say you're struggling with some aspect of business and you've tried everything else and you just can't find the answer. BUT, your grandma makes the best cakes...ever! You could go and get her to teach you how to bake a cake, but look at it through different eyes. Look at it through the eyes of somebody trying to solve a specific business challenge. Ask yourself the question that you need to solve. Recipes and businesses work really well together, incidentally.

You may have all the ingredients but your quantities are wrong. Your recipe might be spot on but the ingredients aren't good enough. You see? Do you see what you can learn? Try it yourself. Think of the problem you're trying to solve and then try to solve it using ideas from a recipe.

Just do anything; whatever catches your eye at that moment. Maybe your child wants you to do some drawing with them. Do it, but keep your challenge in the back of your mind. Let the universe play its part. Be open.

You may have a challenge and you're driving somewhere and you get a puncture. So you start to curse the puncture and get pissed off. Maybe the puncture was a gift. Maybe there was a lesson in the way you change a tyre that you could apply to your business. I don't know. I'm just saying, be open.

Instead of thinking that you are wandering aimlessly from one problem to the next, start thinking that you are being led, by some higher force of goodness, whatever that is for you.

See everything as a gift designed to help you to grow. Even the bad shit.

## What If It's Not Enough?

If you don't find the answers you're looking for and therefore you don't have enough stepping-stones to reach your destination, then do it again. Keep going. Never give in. Somebody somewhere has solved the challenge you're trying to overcome. You just need to keep looking for the answer. You need belief and you need persistence. Keep going.

## Remember The School?

Do you remember the school I told you about where I designed their logo within 2 hours, despite another large design agency struggling for weeks? It's because I believed that I would acquire the new knowledge I would need to solve the problem.

I asked the school what was most important to them. They said it was the fact that they were a Christian School and their connection with the church of the same name.

At that point I knew where to find the answer. I didn't go back to my studio and labor over sheets of ideas. I simply went to the church, KNOWING that their new logo was hidden somewhere. All I had to do was find it. I took my camera with me and in less than half an hour I spotted it. It was a beautiful wrought iron cross, perched at the top of the gable end. It was very distinct and I doubt that many people visiting the church would have ever seen it.

I photographed it, worked it into a simpler form and presented it to the head teacher. He instantly recognized where it was from and said with a big smile "That's it. Done."

What had I done? I had simply acquired new knowledge. First from the head teacher regarding what was important to him, and secondly from the church, which he had told me was most important. And with an expectant, searching mind, I found the answer that I knew I would. I always do. And so will you. Just believe.

## A recap on Step 3: New Knowledge

- Ask your senior executive team first
- Consult with staff to get their input
- Approach select customers and discuss your challenges with them
- Speak to your suppliers for ideas
- Look towards your competitors or even other industries
- Get new knowledge through books, videos, audios and seminars
- Get a business coach
- Think laterally

CHAPTER 6
# STEP 4: TEST

"Never test the depth of river with both feet."

Warren Buffet

So far, we know the problem and where we want to get to, to solve that problem. We've come up with ideas to take us forward and acquired new knowledge to complete the journey. We now believe we've arrived at the outcome we want, but we need to be sure. The only way to be sure is to test.

You've got to get it out there in the world. While ever there's just you and a few associates sat around a table figuring out the answer, not only are you paying them, but there aren't enough of you. Only when you get it out into the real world will you start to get real answers.

I used to be a close-up magician when I was younger, performing at corporate events and weddings. I would practice for hours and hours at home on my own, in front of a mirror, in front of a camera and in front of friends and family. But none of that was real world testing. Only when you get it out there in front of a real audience can you get the real answers you're looking for. Because only in that real scenario do real things happen, such as the kid creeping up behind you and announcing to everyone that he can see a lemon in your hand. The little shit!

It takes a leap of faith to put ideas to the test, but you've got to do it. The other reason it's a great thing to do is because it prepares you for when you come to implement the idea fully. By having already tested it, you've dipped your toe in the water and have begun your momentum toward the final plunge. That is why this step is so significant.

## Limit The Risk

You don't have to test the new idea on all of your customers, all of your staff or all your suppliers.

Let's say for example, you're introducing a new bonus scheme because you think it will improve overall happiness and get you the results that you want. Instead of doing it company wide, just apply it to the next staff who come on board or on the most recent recruits and see what happens. You could even tell them they're being part of a test.

If you're introducing a new payment structure for your customers, rather than hitting them all with it, try it with the next customer who comes through the door and see what the results are.

By testing this way, you are limiting the risk, and it's very easy to reverse or adjust if you get it wrong.

## Look For Criticism

Getting praise is easy. Just show your new idea to those people who love everything you do. But that's not helpful.

You should actively seek criticism. Try and break it. Kick it around and see where the weak bits are. Look for the cracks. Criticism is a gift to help you to grow.

Don't confuse this with complaints and don't confuse it with demands. Maybe a customer doesn't like the new price rise, but that's a complaint rather than a criticism. The policy could still be sound, even if you lose a few customers, so try and read between the lines. Did you know that a price rise of just 10% could result in you requiring a third less customers? So you can make the same amount of money for less effort. The point being, if you lose customers because of a price rise, it doesn't mean it's a bad idea.

The other thing is not to pander to demands either. I know companies who have invested fortunes listening, AND RESPONDING TO, everything their customers say. Jason Fried – founder of 37 Signals - suggests listening to customers but not actioning what they say. He believes that over time, you will begin to hear the same demand being repeated and it will rise above the noise. THAT is the idea you should listen to and take action on.

All I'm saying is encourage criticism. Don't take it personally and don't be quick to react. Just encourage it. Because what is criticism? It's new knowledge. You don't necessarily have to act on that knowledge, but you're richer with it than without it. It gives you a second opinion and one you're not forced to take.

## Split Test

It's easy to think that you know best and you know the right idea when you see it. The right idea isn't the one that you think is right. The right idea is the one that your audience say is right. Let me give you an example.

A client of mine had the challenge of developing a constant flow of new enquiries into his business. So I had a Facebook advertising campaign set up which focused on his core customers. I had 5 different images selected for the advert, which rotated randomly, to see which ones worked best.

After a few days the client called me and told me to take one of the images down because it looked rubbish and didn't give any information over to the audience. Now while I agreed with him, the figures didn't. This one image was getting more clicks than all of the other 4 combined. You can't rely on your own judgment so let the world decide.

## Measure

You need to have some way of measuring the effectiveness of your test and this is tricky. You don't want to carry out the test over too long a period, but you also want the results to be useful. You don't want to carry out tests with too many people in case it's wrong, but too few and you don't get valid answers.

And what do you measure? Let's say you're having financial challenges and you decide to increase your prices by 10%. What are you going to measure here? How happy customers are? Because the chances are they won't be happy. You may in fact lose some customers as a result of this. But as I've already said, does that necessarily matter?

The only thing to measure is whether it takes your business closer to the outcome you really want or further away.

## Take it Into The Future

This is probably my favourite testing technique for ideas and theories. It's something again I learned from Tony Robbins, and it's a fantastic technique, which is based on 'feeling' more than anything else.

The idea is to sit quietly and breathe deeply. Don't breathe into your chest, rather breathe into your stomach. Once you're relaxed, focus on the idea you're thinking of implementing and take yourself into the future with it.

Imagine it's a week's time and the idea's in action. How does that feel? What does it look like? Then take it further into the future in your mind; a month, 3 months, 6 months, 1 year, 10 years. How does it feel now? Does it feel right? Does it feel good? Does it make you feel calm or anxious? Keep breathing and let your mind take you where it wants to take you.

Should you base large decisions on gut instinct and projected future thoughts? My view is that it's as good as any testing technique, if not the best.

I personally have made many large, life-changing decisions using this technique and it has always served me well. Trust yourself.

## What If It's Wrong?

If the results you get back show that you've made a mistake, then you need to go back to Step 2 and get new ideas, and then Step 3 and get new knowledge. At some point between those steps, I would suggest that you have not been rigorous enough. Go deeper. Get the answers you're looking for and then retest. Repeat this process UNTIL you get to the outcome you're looking for. This is where persistence really kicks in. Have you got what it takes to do whatever it takes?

Personally, for me, testing is to gauge whether it feels right. It's not going to give you concrete, conclusive results that will absolutely guarantee success. And nor does it have to.

When we come to make the decision to implement, it's not because the test results PROVED it was right beyond all doubt, but rather because the test results SUGGESTED it was. And look, what we implement next doesn't have to be THE answer. It just has to be better than what we have now. We can always adjust our course because this testing process should be continuous, not a one off.

Testing is like looking at a compass and saying right, that's the destination, has this path taken us further away or closer? Do we need to readjust where we're heading or do we need to put our foot down and implement? Just keep stopping and keep checking. Keep asking "Are we on track? Are we on target? Are we on schedule?" Keep making those incremental adjustments you need to keep heading in the right direction.

## A recap on Step 4: Test

- Limit the risk by using a small testing sample
- Actively look for criticism
- Split test so you have results to compare
- Develop an appropriate way to measure the results
- Project the idea into the future and see what it feels like

CHAPTER 7
# STEP 5: IMPLEMENT

"Knowing is not enough;

we must apply."

Bruce Lee

If you have worked through the process so far with belief and persistence, you should now have an idea that you believe should take you to your destination. So now is the time to implement that idea. Another word you could use is to 'activate' the idea.

Unless you implement the idea and make it active, it is totally worthless and useless.

The mistake people can make at this stage is to hold off making the decision to implement. They are worried about making the wrong decision and so they end up making no decision. But the irony of that is that they ARE in fact making a decision – they're deciding NOT to decide.

But this doesn't have to be the last decision you ever make. Let me say that again. THIS DOESN'T HAVE TO BE THE LAST DECISION YOU EVER MAKE. The point being that even if you make the wrong decision, you can always make another one.

The other thing to consider is the cost of reversing a decision. It's often not as costly or as difficult to change a decision as you may think.

All that said, it's important to trust in the process and to trust in your ability to decide. Now is the time to be brave and to act. It's time to implement and activate your idea. It's time to take the leap and very often the universe will demand that leap. It will rarely be a comfortable step. The universe needs to know that you're committed to the idea and that you believe in it yourself. So it will set the final stepping-stone just slightly too far from your goal. The final stepping-stone in your journey will in fact be a leaping-stone. Know this. Anticipate this, because here we go. It's time to leap.

"Leap and grow your wings on the way down."

Les Brown

Obviously I'm having to talk very generally because I don't know you're problem or your solution. So not all of this will be relevant. But let me give you some ideas that work for a range of scenarios.

## I Have Several Ideas To Implement

You may have arrived at several ideas that could all solve your problem. Throughout the process, you may have actually generated several ideas to drive your business forward beyond the point you were trying to get to. So your new challenge now is to decide which ones to implement first.

If this is the case, you need to have a way of deciding which ones to go with, and in what order. Having loads of great ideas and not implementing any is worse than having no ideas. So here are some questions you can use to help you to decide which ideas to run with first. So I would be asking myself, which one:

- Is going to give me the best results for the least effort?
- Is easy to implement?
- Demands the least time?
- Could I get other people to do?
- Do we have the skills to do?
- Costs the least?
- Is the lowest risk?
- Aligns with our long-term goals?

## Launch Version 1.0

Many people get so caught up in trying to make everything perfect that they never get it into the world. The trick that masters use is to make it good enough and to implement it. Have you ever had a software update on your phone? What version of Microsoft Word are you using?

If companies had to wait until everything was perfect, they'd never do anything.

To get your idea to 75% good enough, might take a week. To get it to 85% good enough might take another month. 95% might take another year and then to take it to 99% might take another 5 years. To go from 99% to 100% may take 20 years. Do you see how much time is taken up in those last percentage improvements?

For me, get it out the door at 75%. Get it above ground and working for your business. The speed at which it will then improve will accelerate because there are more people contributing to its development...for free! Get your customers using version 1.0 and paying for it. They will then give you all the feedback you need to take it to version 1.1, 1.2 etc. and it won't cost you a penny for their comments.

Is there a risk in using this approach? Yes, but it's far riskier to keep it under wraps until it's perfect because the danger of that route is that it may NEVER see the light of day. Or worse, someone beats you to it.

## Start Now

You've got to get this idea moving. It's like trying to push a car: those first yards are tough, but once it's rolling it's much easier. So it's important that while you're pumped-up about the idea that you get things moving straight away.

Who can you call? What do you need to buy? What meeting do you need to arrange? Whatever you need to do, take immediate steps towards implementation as soon as you decide it's the right thing for you.

And the amount of energy you need to get it started is not the same amount of energy you need to get it over the line. That requires a different type of energy. The energy a rocket needs to get off the ground and through the atmosphere is far greater than the energy needed to take it the rest of the way to the moon.

## Take Massive Action

When you decide to implement, you've got to take massive action. Whatever it is you're about to do, I guarantee it will take 10 times more effort than you thought it would. You've got to be prepared for this and take massive, unreasonable, relentless action towards your goal.

Read "The 10X Rule" by Grant Cardone if you need some mental fuel to get you through this stage.

Get more people. Allow for more time. Muster more strength. Know why you're doing this. Get your head down and give it whatever it takes. WHATEVER IT TAKES. Just decide. And make it yours.

## Produce the Procedure

Whatever it is you're doing, produce the procedure. This will create a system and strategy for implementing it correctly every single time, again and again. This procedure can be as simple as a checklist.

If the challenge you've overcome is something that needs to be overcome continually, then you most certainly need a procedure. For example, let's say your problem is not having enough customers buying from you, when you meet them. You might generate a series of steps you are going to take next time to wow them and to get them to buy from you. You therefore need to write a procedure, a strategy, a policy, a system, a checklist, whatever you call it, so that it will be done the same way EVERY SINGLE TIME.

But even if it is something that solves a one-off problem, I would still say to `procedurise`. Let's say you apply the Pink Tie Principle and conclude that your boyfriend is a dick and he needs to go. You might want to take five minutes out of your day to produce the procedure for selecting your next boyfriend, or the Exit Strategy Procedure, which kicks in when he starts being a dick. I put this in half jokingly, but just to demonstrate that seemingly one-off decisions will need to be made again at some point in the future.

## Set The Procedure in Stone

What are you going to do to enforce this procedure? How you are you going to cement the idea in the minds of your team, your clients, your suppliers and most importantly, yourself?

Do you have a handbook? A company bible that explains how to do everything? You should. If you do, put it in there.

As well as creating handbooks, I also get my clients to produce a Golden Rules handbook, which pulls out the MOST important procedures so that everyone can be reminded of them.

With some clients, I create posters for them of their most important procedures. THE most important one I sometimes have framed in 4ft high gold gilded frames.

You could in fact have them carved in stone. (I've never done that but wouldn't it be great?)

You may want to declare them publically on your website if that makes sense. Whatever you need to do, set them in the minds of the people they affect the most.

## Train The Procedure

The people who this procedure affects then need training in it, and not just as a one off, but continually. So set up a training schedule for this new system or way of doing things. Make sure the people it affects know it inside and out. Train it in different scenarios, then retrain and train again.

Get your team to train others in how it should be done because teaching it really cements the ideas in.

In Goshinkwai we would train the same attack over and over again. We would train it slowly and fast, with big people and small people. We would train it wearing different clothes and with our eyes shut. We would even have people screaming obscenities whilst growling and spitting throughout the attack. This led to our response being automatic because we drilled it over and over again. Do you think I would be in a stronger position to defend this attack over someone who had never experienced it before?

Make training fun, turn it into a game if possible. Whatever you do, this new way of doing things must become engrained and second nature to those it affects. You don't want it to be another one of those faddy ideas you came up with, which people dismissed once your back was turned. You don't want your team to be caught off guard. Drill and train your procedures in every scenario you can imagine.

## Set The Rules

You might even put rules in place about this new way of doing things. What will happen if they don't do it this way? Tell them upfront. Manage their expectations.

At the end of the day, this is YOUR business and so everything must be done YOUR way.

Set the rules. Make them clear, make them fair, but most importantly, make them.

## Don't expect anyone to like it

The World Health Organisation commissioned a study into how they could reduce deaths during operations. Atul Gawande headed this up in conjunction with specialists from the airline industry. What they came up with was checklists. These checklists included simple things like:
- Do you know what side of the body you're operating on?
- Does everybody know each other's name?
- Have you washed your hands properly?

When they implemented these simple checklists, death rates were cut by almost half.

But when they asked the nurses and Doctors whether they were happy about using the new checklists, most of them said NO. However, then they asked that if THEY were being operated on, how many of them would want the operating staff to use the checklists, and they all said YES.

Don't expect anyone to like YOUR checklists. And don't care either. Set them in stone and make them happen.

## Control The Quality

I know what it's like. You have a great idea, which you implement. You create the procedure and train people in how to deliver it. Everyone loves it and sticks to it...for a while. Then at some point they stop.

Remember that if you EXPECT something, you've got INSPECT that something.

This doesn't have to be done by you. You may have a manager or supervisor in place to carry out that role, and it's their job to report in to you so you know everything is getting done EVERY SINGLE TIME.

That's the key. What do you have to do to make sure it gets done every time? This is where procedures and the greatest ideas fail. They fall between the gaps and gather dust rather than generate cash for you.

It's in this level of implementation where the massive action kicks in. People get the idea in place but then fail to take these final steps to cement that idea in place and to make sure it gets delivered, perfectly, every single time, forever more.

If you are not prepared to take your idea to this level, don't bother actioning it in the first place because it will always be a waste of effort.

"You can expect what you inspect."

W. Edwards Deming

## A recap on Step 5: Implement

- Decide to take action
- Start straight away with what you have, where you are and get momentum.
- Resign yourself to taking massive action.
- Produce the procedure
- Set the procedure in stone
- Train the procedure and make sure everyone knows your rules
- Don't expect anyone to like the checklist and don't care either.
- Inspect the outcome you want

CHAPTER 8
# STEP 6: EVOLVE

"Commit to constant and never-ending improvement."

Tony Robbins

Adopting the mindset to constantly evolve and improve something is the one thing that will take you to the very top and make you untouchable and unstoppable.

Let me use an analogy. Would you rather I gave you £100,000 today or a penny today, which doubles in value every day for just 30 days; so tomorrow it's worth a 2p, the day after 4p and so on. Which would you choose?

The answer is that after just 30 days of doubling the penny, it becomes worth £10.7million.

The point is that with small improvements on a disciplined, regular basis, the results grow exponentially and are staggering.

People don't understand the power of the compound effect and constantly look for the big win. They don't realize that small, daily wins, quickly add up.

When people try and lose weight, they go on crash diets and hammer the gym for a few weeks. This is unsustainable and the irony is that if they were to just make minor adjustments to their eating habits, drink more water and lightly exercise for just 10 minutes each morning, overtime, the results would be amazing. The important part of this process is DISCIPLINE.

Take the example of the penny which doubles everyday for a month that turns into £10.7million. Let's say you took just the weekends off and only doubled the penny on weekdays. The final amount after 30 days, would be less than £10,500. So for only a small sacrifice in discipline, the results are vastly affected. And so is the case in life and in business.

"There are two types of pain you will go through in life, the pain of discipline or the pain of regret."

Jim Rohn

## Evolve Your Ideas

Now that you have implemented your idea and have developed a procedurised, systemised way for delivering the same outcome, consistently every time, we are now in a position to evolve it

You've got version 1.0 out of the door which is great, but we must be upgrading it to 1.1, 1.2 and so on, with some regularity.

Let's say your challenge was that you had a low conversion rate when meeting potential clients, something like 10%. So the outcome you developed was a set procedure for your sales team to work to, every time they go and meet a potential new client. And let's say you instantly manage to increase your conversion rate to 20%. The procedure and training is critical because we must be performing with some regularity otherwise we will never be able to maintain or improve it. Once the consistency's there, we then have a base to work on and improve.

So in month one, I would be asking how can we improve that to 21%. The process I would go through is that which has already been outlined, in that I would come up with new ideas, acquire new knowledge, split test the outcomes and then implement the winning ones into my procedure. And repeat... forevermore.

For example, you might try taking a box of donuts with you to half the meetings and none to the other half. Once you find that the donut idea improves your conversion rate, this must then be cemented into the procedure and everyone needs training in this new step.

Somebody must be assigned to take responsibility for developing the process. They must schedule time aside EVERY MONTH at least, to be working ON evolving this process rather IN delivering it. Does that make sense?

This policy should be adopted by everybody within your company and across everything you do. This principle is taken to the highest degrees in Japan, with their highly pursued 'Kaizen'.

## Kaizen

Kaizen is a Japanese word, which in business has become to mean 'continual improvement'. It is a discipline, which is adopted by everybody within an organization on a daily basis.

After World War II, when Japanese industry was at rock bottom, American experts were brought in to help rebuild industry and in-turn, the country. Professor, engineer and statistician Dr Edwards Deming brought the idea of constant, daily improvement into the businesses he helped and it became termed in Japan as 'kaizen'.

This simple philosophy of small, daily improvements done by everybody, helped turn non-existent companies into global giants. These companies have seen many years of continual success around the world.

The question to be asking yourself is "How can I do this better than I did it yesterday?'" Just imagine if EVERYONE in your organisation was doing this.

Because the reality is that if you're not improving something, it's getting worse. If you're not growing, you're shrinking. If you're not evolving, you're devolving.

Furthermore, if you're growing, you are truly living and will approach each day with enthusiasm and vibrancy.

Just imagine, rather than your team turning up and performing the same mundane tasks, they're coming in and thinking how can I make this better? How can I be better? Imagine going home every single day, being better than the last. Imagine having all of your staff making small, daily, weekly or monthly improvements in their area. Can you imagine what impact this would have on your business over time? And where does it start? With you!

"If you will change, everything will change for you."

Jim Rohn

## How To Evolve

There are many ways in which an implemented idea can evolve. The way you evolve the idea is again in the questions you ask and the following actions you then take. Here is a series of questions you could use to evolve your ideas:

- How could I make it easier to do?
- How could I make it faster?
- How could I make it cheaper?
- How could I make it simpler?
- How could I make it more enjoyable?
- How could I do it and give more value?
- How can this take us closer towards our long-term goals?

Another great way to evolve is through Split Testing, which I have mentioned previously. Now this only works if you have sufficient data to support the tests. The way split testing works is to make just ONE change at a time, and to test one half of events with the change and the other one without. If you make more than one change at once, you will never know which one had the greatest impact.

If all you did were test a new idea each month and then use the findings to evolve the system, there would be no stopping you. You will be constantly growing and your competitors will be constantly playing catch-up, and before they know it, it will be all over.

## Are You Committed to the Evolution?

Are you committed to this idea of evolving, or is it going to be just another of those good ideas that get's shelved with the rest?

What are you going to do to implement this idea company-wide? How are you going to train your team in it? How are you going to remember to do it with great consistency? How are you going to create the time and space to allow this to happen? Who do you need to help you to make this happen? Who is going to check that this is happening?

Out of everything you've ever learnt, this is the ONE thing that will make sense of EVERYTHING you've ever learnt.

This is the one thing that deserves your commitment to make part of the culture and nature of everything you do.

This is the one thing that has the power to change your life, your relationships, your body, your business, your wealth and your happiness.

Make a commitment to yourself to make this a lifelong discipline you are going to work hard to form into a habit, because if you don't, I promise you with great certainty that you will look back with regret on what you COULD have achieved.

This is where everything changes for you; your business and your success. It's time to join the evolution!

## A recap on Step 6: Evolve

- Understand the power of making continual improvements
- Evolve everything, every day
- Get your entire company to adopt the philosophy of Kaizen
- Start making continual improvements yourself, on a daily basis

## CHAPTER 9
# THE BEGINNING

"If you are going through hell, keep going. Never, never, never give up."

Winston Churchill

The Pink Tie Principle itself has evolved and I'm sure will continue to do so.

Over the years I have simplified, reduced and improved the process to what I have presented to you here.

By adopting this principle in most everything I do, I am able to approach situations with a great sense of calm and knowing that I will surmount the challenge I face, and will be able to turn it into a great opportunity.

This has raised my levels of optimism to what people might describe as irritating because while others are becoming overwhelmed at the challenges they face, I am able to adopt a solid stance that will see me through.

My greatest wish is that you are able to see each challenge as a gift to grow and that you are able to arm yourself with the Pink Tie Principle to overcome the challenges that arise. I hope that you may enjoy the success that you so dearly deserve that is waiting for you on the other side.

Remember, you are being led. Try not to judge things as good or bad, they just are. See them as gifts to grow and I will see you beyond the top.

# INSPIRATION

Over the years so many incredible people have inspired me through their seminars, videos and books. Lots of them reinforce what each other say, so it can be difficult to attribute sources of inspiration specifically. So here is a list of people who I would suggest you make it your mission to discover, for their words are far greater than mine. Find their videos, buy their books, download their audiobooks, attend their seminars and devour everything they have:

- Tony Robbins
- Grant Cardone
- Seth Godin
- Les Brown
- Zig Ziglar
- Jim Rohn
- Timothy Ferris
- Edward de Bono
- Brendon Burchard
- W. Edwards Deming

## ABOUT THE AUTHOR

James Ashford is an inspirational and motivational business mentor, speaker and in his own words 'rocker of worlds'.

He works with leading businesses to help take them beyond their current challenges and towards the greatest ambitions they have for their company. He also works very closely with business owners and their executive teams to help remove their limiting beliefs and get them motivated & fired-up to succeed.

James is constantly studying the world's greatest companies and individuals to discover how they've succeeded, which he melds with his passion & inspiration and shares with his client's and fans.

He authors a successful business blog at **www.JamesAshford.com**, which you can subscribe to for free and where he continually shares his best content.

James also delivers Business Mastery & Breakthrough Workshops and Seminars throughout the year and provides the same content via online programs at **www.MasteryPrograms.com**.

To find out more information about this book or to leave a personal comment for James, visit **www.PinkTiePrinciple.com**.

## NOTE FROM THE AUTHOR

Thank you so much for reading my book. I really appreciate your purchase and I am grateful that you have invested your precious time to read it.

If you've enjoyed this book and have found at least one idea that has affected your thinking or could move your business forward, then please leave a review wherever you bought it.

Books make great gifts and a lot of readers choose to buy copies of 'The Pink Tie Principle' for their friends and colleagues. For bulk purchases please visit **www.PinkTiePrinciple.com**.

I would also love for you to get in touch with me personally, whether that's through one of my websites or via Twitter @THEJamesAshford. I always enjoy hearing your feedback.

I genuinely wish you all the very best for the future and hope that you continue to smash through your challenges and find the success you deserve on the other side.

Thank you,

Printed in Great Britain
by Amazon